AF480550

Hex codes, or hexadecimal codes, are a way to represent colors in digital devices and web design. Each hex code refers to a very specific color. A hex color is expressed as a six-digit combination of numbers and letters, preceded by a pound sign or hashtag, defined by its mix of red, green, and blue (RGB). The first two letters or numbers refer to red, the next two refer to green, and the last two refer to blue.

The color values are defined as values between 00 and FF. Hex codes are a universal way to describe colors. This book is specifically about shades of green.

A is for alien armpit

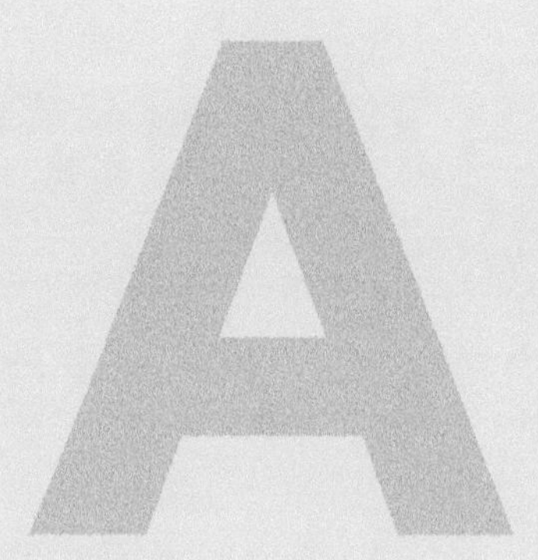

#84DE02

a is for apple green

a

#8DB600

B is for bahai

B

#A5CB0C

b is for bamboo green

b

#52914A

C is for camarone

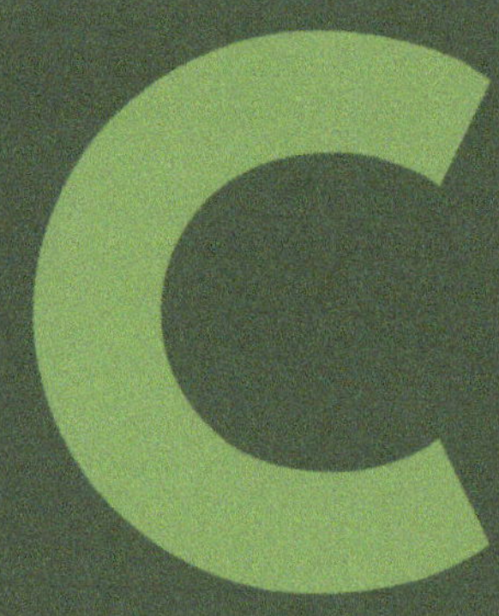

#00581A

c is for christi

c

#67A120

D is for de york

D

#7AC488

d is for dell

d

#396413

E is for elf green

E

#088370

e is for elm green

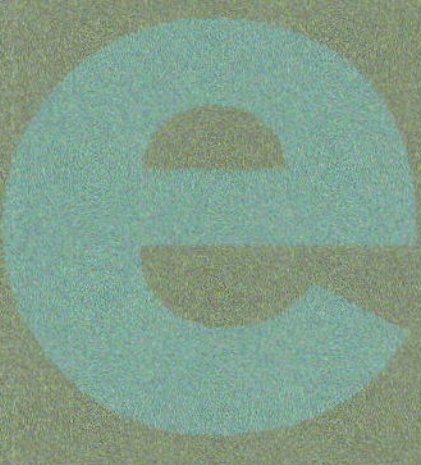

#5F8144

F is for fairy tails forest

F

#008000

f is for fern

f

#63B76C

G is for gossip green

G

#9FD385

g is for groovy

g

#5CA345

H is for happy hour

H

#A9C949

h is for highland

h

#6F8E63

I is for iguana green

I

#71BC78

i is for ivy green 2

#1D711B

J is for juice green

J

#C0D036

j is for june bud

#BDDA57

K is for kirchner green

K

#5C6116

k is for kiwi green

k

#ABBA3B

L is for la palma

#368716

l is for limeade

l

#6F9D02

M is for mantis

M

#74C365

m is for may green

m

#4C9141

N is for napier green

N

#2A8000

n is for neon lime green

n

#82D059

O is for olivetone

#716E10

o is for oregano green

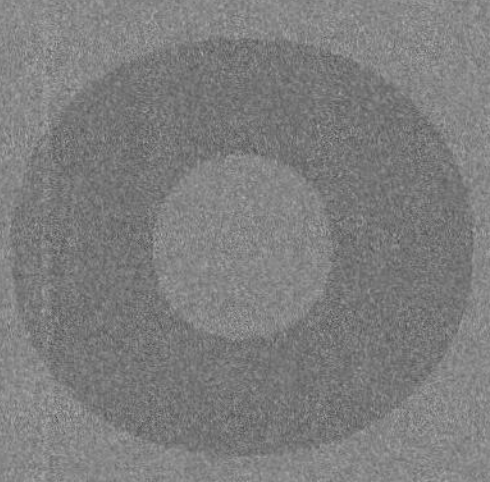

#4F7949

P is for peppermint

P

#379503

p is for pistachio

p

#93C572

Q is for quacking grass

#BFC2A1

q is for quartz green

q

#6E7C45

R is for rain forest

R

#667028

r is for reindeer moss

r

#BDBB6E

S is for sap green

S

#507D2A

s is for seaweed

s

#003A1E

T is for top secret

T

#7AAC21

t is for trendy green

t

#7C881A

U is for universal green

U

#006B38

u is for usumo'egi

U

#8DB255

V is for verdun green

V

#495400

v is for vesuvian green

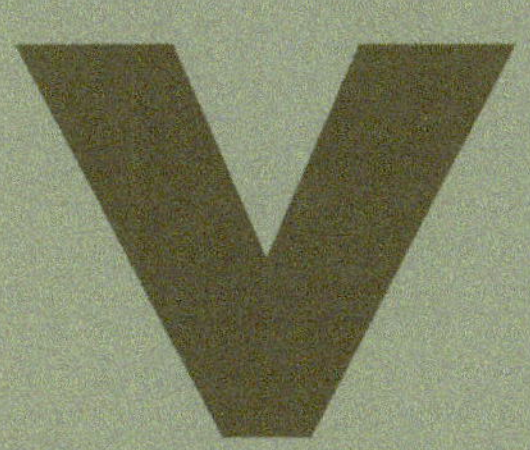

#879860

W is for watercourse

W

#056F57

w is for wild willow

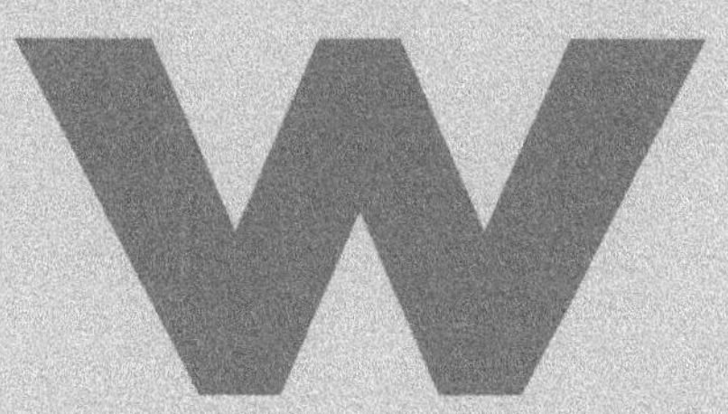

#B9C46A

X is for xl aged copper

X

#90AA93

x is for x-75 soft green

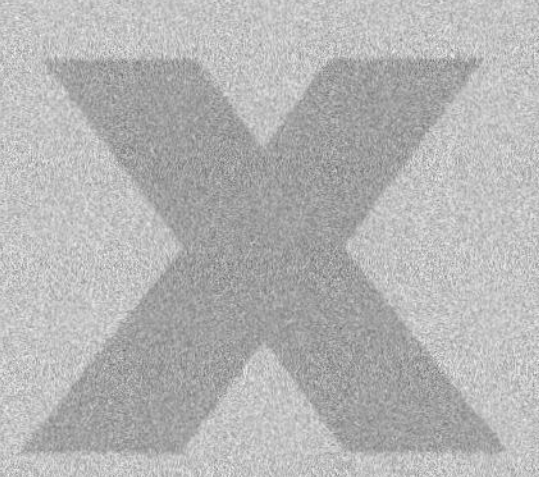

#BDC2A4

Y is for yanagizome

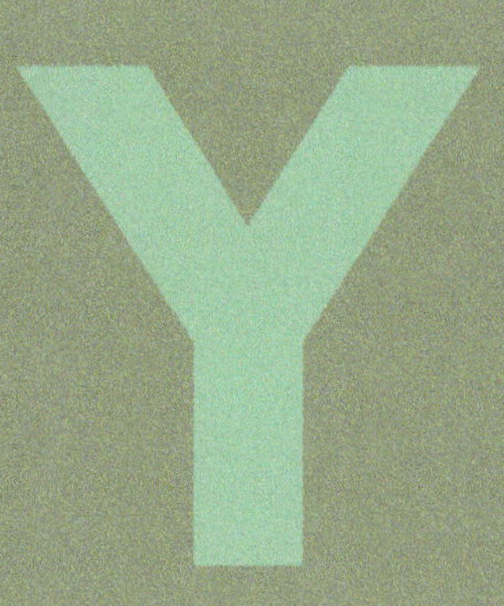

#8C9E5E

y is for yardline

y

#60BB75

Z is for zephyr green

#83AC82

z is for zestful

Z

#94B57F